Platform Maths 2

Liz Hopkins

Leopard Learning

Mary Hayward. (written upside down)

Leopard Learning

Find out more about our books

If you would like to find out more about our books, simply complete and return this photocopiable form with a large stamped addressed envelope

Name _____

Address _____

_____

_____

_____ Postcode _____

Please return to: *Leopard Learning*, P.O. Box 43, Stroud, GL6 7YA
Don't forget the large stamped addressed envelope!

Text ©Liz Hopkins 1997
Illustrations © Leopard Learning 1997
First published by Leopard Learning Ltd, PO Box 2271, Bath, BA2 6RU, 1997. Reprinted 2000

The right of Liz Hopkins to be identified as the author of this work has been asserted by her in accordance with the Copyright, Designs and Patents Act 1988.

The copyright holders authorise ONLY users of Platform Maths Calculations to make photocopies or stencil duplicates of the copymasters for their own or their classes' immediate use within the teaching context.

No other rights are granted without permission in writing from the publishers or under license from the Copyright Licensing Agency Limited. Further details of such licenses (for reprographic reproduction) may be obtained from the Copyright Licensing Agency Limited, 90 Tottenham Court Road, London W1P 9HE.

Copy by any other means or for any other purpose is strictly prohibited without the prior written consent of the copyright holders. Applications for such permission should be addressed to the publishers.

A catalogue record for this book is available from the British Library.

ISBN 1 899929 15 0

Typeset by Leopard Learning Ltd, Bath

Printed in Great Britain by Redwood Books Ltd, Trowbridge

Introduction

Platform Maths provides the extensive, structured practice of the core number skills that so many children need. It has a clear mathematical structure, small learning steps and strong reinforcement at every stage to consolidate basic skills. *Platform Maths 1-3* focuses on the core number and algebra required for Levels 1, 2 and Working towards Level 3 of The National Curriculum, and Scottish Levels A-B in exceptional detail. The books are designed to be used on their own or alongside your core maths scheme or scheme of work, and for both Key Stage 1 and Key Stage 2 children and for older special needs pupils.

The key features of Platform Maths are as follows:
- it concentrates on the crucial number skills in a continuum of learning. The maths development is based upon a common progression of learning which will be broadly similar to the sequence of your core maths scheme.
- each book provides about 90 carefully structured and graded photocopiable practice sheets.
- number is broken down into small steps so that there are no big leaps in learning.
- lots of varied practice of each new step means that learning is always reinforced.
- the artwork style has been deliberately developed to cater for both younger children and older special needs pupils. It aims to avoid a limited age-appeal whilst remaining lively and appealing.
- there is a low reading age. The use of the 'rebus' device helps slower readers with unusual nouns.
- nearly every sheet provides an extension activity marked with this logo: , which provides extra practice, differentiation for children working faster, and an assessment of learning.
- every sheet provides considerable practice of a skill to make your journey to the photocopier worthwhile and cost-effective.
- an amusing reward icon has been included at the bottom of each page to provide a highly enjoyable incentive to success in learning. The reward icons can be coloured if the sheet is completed correctly, or cut out and collected on a record sheet (see *Free Resources*).
- Resource sheets are provided at the back to enable you to create your own further sheets to consolidate any area of number which you feel needs even more reinforcement. Sheets which can be directly followed up with a blank resource sheet are marked with a logo like this: which also indicates the letter of the relevant resource sheet.

About Platform Maths 2

This book follows on directly from **Platform Maths 1**, covering most of Level 2 of the National Curriculum for number, Scottish Guidelines 5-14 Levels A-B. It starts with eight practice sheets which consolidate addition and subtraction to 10 and which can be used to encourage mental recall of this learning. Its major focus is on place value to 100 and add and subtract to 20, and includes substantial work on counting in twos, fives and tens, the start of sequences and early multiplication and division skills. You will also find a valuable block of number problems (sheets 61-66) to consolidate addition and subtraction in context. Each step has at least two photocopiable sheets and some have more than ten. You will find the exact maths progression set out on the next two pages, correlated to the National Curriculum. You can also use this contents page as a record sheet. Use this contents and the small maths headings at the top of each page to identify the maths covered.

Suggestions for using the book

- **alongside your maths scheme**: rarely does a published scheme offer enough variety and consolidation for all pupils; this resource supplies extra practice in a range of contexts to enrich children's experience and increase their grasp of number. This resource gives a range of clear, easily accessible practice sheets which can be worked through or dipped into as you judge necessary. A correlation for every major maths scheme is available from Leopard Learning (see *Free Resources* on the previous page).

- **for special needs**: the amusing but age-neutral artwork and the use of rebus features have been specially designed to make the sheets useful for a very wide age range. They carry no visual 'message' to make them babyish to older children, and the depth of consolidation makes them ideal for slower learners who need small steps and repeated reinforcement.

- **for making up workbooks of your own**: you can select sheets to make up your own number workbooks and a free photocopiable workbook cover is available from the publishers for this purpose (see *Free Resources*)

- **using the reward feature**: as explained above this can be used in numerous ways to develop tremendous motivation to 'get them all right'. A special photocopiable reward booklet is available from the publishers if you wish children to collect the pictures (see *Free Resources*). If you do not wish to use the feature, simply photocopy a master sheet and stick a blank square over the picture.

- **for assessment**: use the extra activity at the bottom of the page, which can be answered in the pupil's maths book, as an assessment of the learning on the sheet. Photocopy the contents pages to record progress.

Answers

Free answer sheets are available from Leopard Learning (see *Free Resources*).

Resources

Few special resources are needed to use these sheets, but the following pieces of simple maths equipment are mentioned in the text:

- up to 20 plastic cubes (or similar) for practical addition and subtraction.
- a set of cards numbered 0-9. Either make your own or send for a free photocopiable sheet. (See *Free Resources*.)

Contents and record sheet

Name _____

Sheet No	Maths covered	National Curriculum coverage (POS)
1	Addition practice: up to 10	*know addition and subtraction facts to 20…(3c)*
2	Addition practice: up to 10	
3	Addition practice: bonds of 10	
4	Addition practice: bonds of 10	
5	Subtraction practice: up to 10	
6	Subtraction practice: up of 10	
7	Subtraction practice: bonds of 10	
8	Subtraction practice: bonds of 10	
9	Numbers to 50: numerals	*count orally up to 10 and beyond, knowing the number names…(2a)*
10	Numbers to 50: numerals	
11	Numbers to 50: counting	
12	Numbers to 50: counting	
13	Numbers to 50: ordering	*read, write and order numbers, initially to 10, progressing up to 1000…(2b)*
14	Numbers to 50: ordering	
15	Numbers to 50: counting on	*understand the operations of addition, subtraction as taking away and comparison…(4a)*
16	Numbers to 50: counting on	
17	Numbers to 50: counting back	
18	Numbers to 50: counting back	
19	Pre-multiplication: counting on	*understand the operations of multiplication, and division as sharing and repeated subtraction…(4b)*
20	Pre-multiplication: grouping	
21	Pre-division: counting back	
22	Pre-division: sharing	
23	Extending patterns: what comes next?	*use repeating patterns to develop ideas of regularity and sequencing…(3a)*
24	Extending patterns: what comes next?	
25	Number sequences: counting in 2s	*learn multiplication and division facts relating to 2s, 5s, 10s, and use these to learn other facts…(3c)*
26	Number sequences: counting in 2s	
27	Number sequences: counting in 2s	
28	Number sequences: multiples of 2	
29	Number sequences: counting in 5s	
30	Number sequences: counting in 5s	
31	Number sequences: counting in 5s	
32	Number sequences: multiples of 5	
33	Number sequences: multiples of 2 and 5	
34	Number sequences: counting in 10s	
35	Number sequences: counting in 10s	
36	Addition to 20: adding units	*know addition and subtraction facts to 20…(3c)*
37	Addition to 20: adding units	
38	Addition to 20: adding 10	
39	Addition to 20: adding 10	

40	Addition to 20: over the 10 boundary	*know addition and subtraction facts to 20…(3c)*
41	Addition to 20: over the 10 boundary	
42	Addition to 20: subtracting units	
43	Subtraction to 20: subtracting units	
44	Subtraction to 20: subtracting 10	
45	Subtraction to 20: subtracting 10	
46	Subtraction to 20: over the 10 boundary	
47	Subtraction to 20: over the 10 boundary	
48	Addition to 20: number facts	
49	Addition to 20: number facts	
50	Addition to 20: number facts	
51	Subtraction to 20: number facts	
52	Subtraction to 20: number facts	
53	Subtraction to 20: number facts	
54	Place value: up to 19	*developing an understanding that the position of a digit signifies its value…(2b)*
55	Place value: up to 19	
56	Place value: up to 19	
57	Place value: up to 19	
58	Place value: up to 50	
59	Place value: up to 50	
60	Place value: up to 50	
61	Number problems: addition	*recognise situations to which they (addition and subtraction) apply and use them to solve problems…(4a)*
62	Number problems: addition	
63	Number problems: subtraction	
64	Number problems: subtraction	
65	Number problems: addition and subtraction	
66	Number problems: addition and subtraction	
67	Numbers to 100: ordering	*read, write and order numbers, initially to 10, progressing up to 1000…(2b)*
68	Numbers to 100: ordering	
69	Numbers to 100: ordering	
70	Numbers to 100: ordering	
71	Numbers to 100: ordering	
72	Numbers to 100: ordering	
73	Number sequences: counting in 10s	*learn multiplication and division facts relating to the…10s…(3c)*
74	Number sequences: counting in 10s	
75	Number sequences: multiples of 10	
76	Place value: up to 100	*developing an understanding that the position of a digit signifies its value…(2b)*
77	Place value: up to 100	
78	Place value: adding 10	
79	Place value: adding 10	
80	Place value: adding 10	
81	Place value: taking 10	
82	Place value: taking 10	
83	Place value: difference	

Resource sheets A-F

1

Addition practice: Up to 10

Name _____

Join to the right answer.

(4 / 6 / 7) +1 (7 / 5 / 8)   (3 / 6 / 8) +2 (10 / 5 / 8)

(4 / 2 / 6) +4 (8 / 10 / 6)   (7 / 3 / 5) +3 (6 / 8 / 10)

(4 / 2 / 3) +6 (8 / 10 / 9)   (3 / 5 / 4) +5 (8 / 9 / 10)

(6 / 2 / 4) +3 (9 / 7 / 5)   (5 / 3 / 6) +4 (7 / 9 / 10)

Addition practice: Up to 10

Name _____

2 more

7 → ☐
5 → ☐
3 → ☐
6 → ☐
8 → ☐

1 more

6 → ☐
4 → ☐
9 → ☐
7 → ☐
5 → ☐

3 more

6 → ☐
4 → ☐
7 → ☐
5 → ☐
3 → ☐

4 more

5 → ☐
2 → ☐
3 → ☐
6 → ☐
4 → ☐

3

Name _____

Addition practice: Bonds of 10

Complete the number sentences.

4 + 6 = ☐   8 + ☐ = 10

6 + ☐ = 10   2 + 8 = ☐

1 + 9 = ☐   3 + 7 = ☐

☐ + 1 = 10   ☐ + 3 = 10

5 + ☐ = 10   4 + ☐ = 10

5 + 5 = ☐   6 + 4 = ☐

10 + 0 = ☐   7 + 3 = ☐

0 + ☐ = 10   ☐ + 7 = 10

4

Addition practice: Bonds of 10

Name _____

Colour ▢▢ cards that make 10.

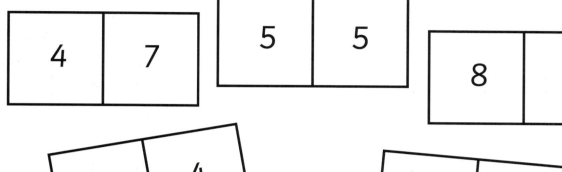

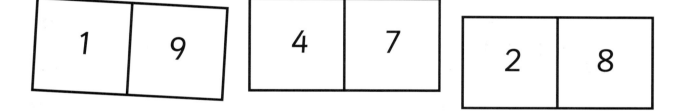
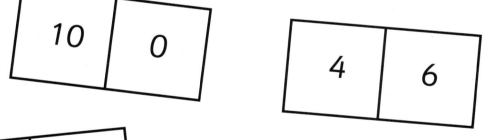
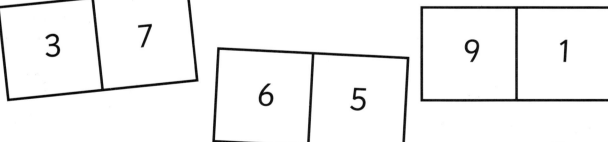

5

Name _____

Subtraction practice: Up to 10

Complete the number sentences.

9 - 8 = ☐   3 - 2 = ☐

7 - 1 = ☐   5 - 4 = ☐

8 - 5 = ☐   6 - 3 = ☐

10 - 9 = ☐   4 - 1 = ☐

4 - 2 = ☐   10 - 10 = ☐

6 - 3 = ☐   3 - 1 = ☐

4 - 4 = ☐   6 - 5 = ☐

9 - 7 = ☐   7 - 5 = ☐

7 - 6 = ☐   5 - 2 = ☐

Subtraction practice: Bonds of 10

Name _____

Join the flower to the right pot.

7

Subtraction practice: Bonds of 10

Name _____

Match the sums to the right answers.

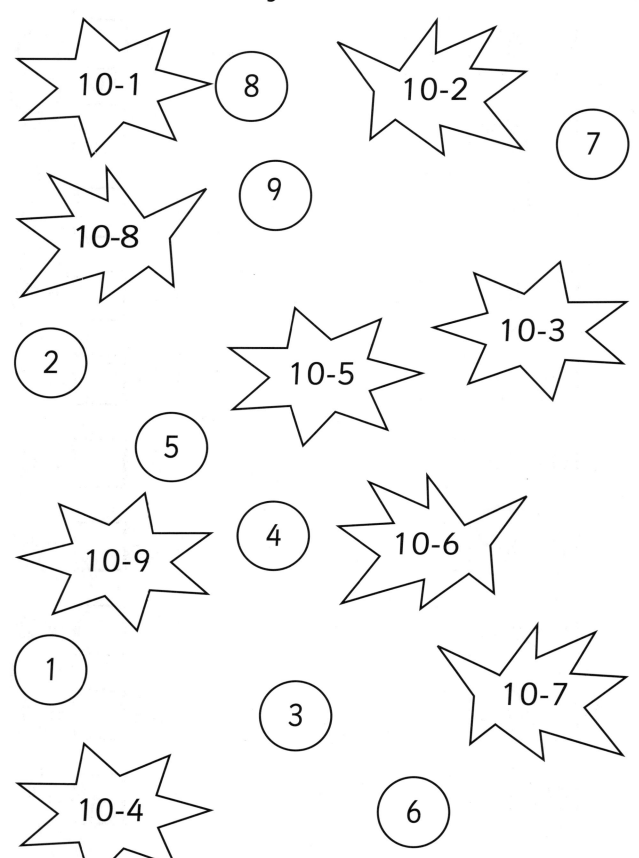

8 PLATFORM MATHS

Name _____

Subtraction practice: Bonds of 10

10 - 4 = ☐   10 - ☐ = 10

10 - 9 = ☐   10 - ☐ = 6

10 - 0 = ☐   10 - ☐ = 3

10 - 5 = ☐   10 - ☐ = 1

10 - 7 = ☐   10 - ☐ = 7

10 - 3 = ☐   10 - ☐ = 0

10 - 1 = ☐   10 - ☐ = 5

10 - 6 = ☐   10 - ☐ = 2

10 - 10 = ☐   10 - ☐ = 4

10 - 2 = ☐   10 - ☐ = 9

Numbers to 50: Numerals

Name _____

Fill in the missing numbers.

 Start at 19, then 37, then 41.
Write the next 5 numbers each time.

Well done!

 **10**

Numbers to 50: Numerals

Name _____

Fill in the missing numbers.

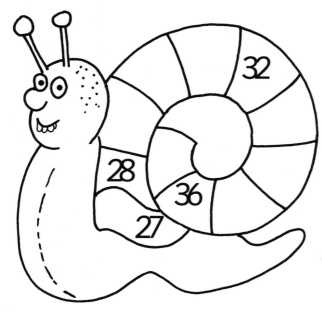
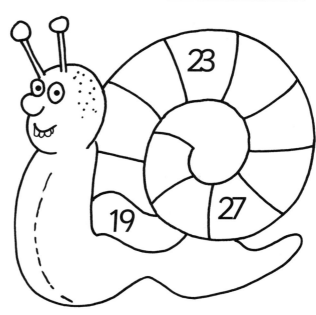
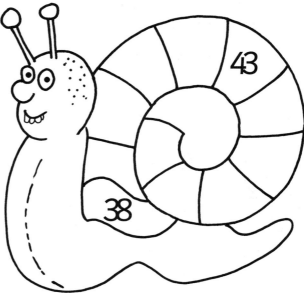
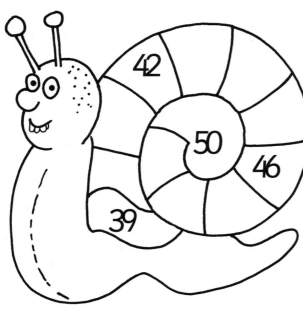

 Write a number line from 1 to 50.

Well done!

11

How many?

Name _____

Numbers to 50: Counting

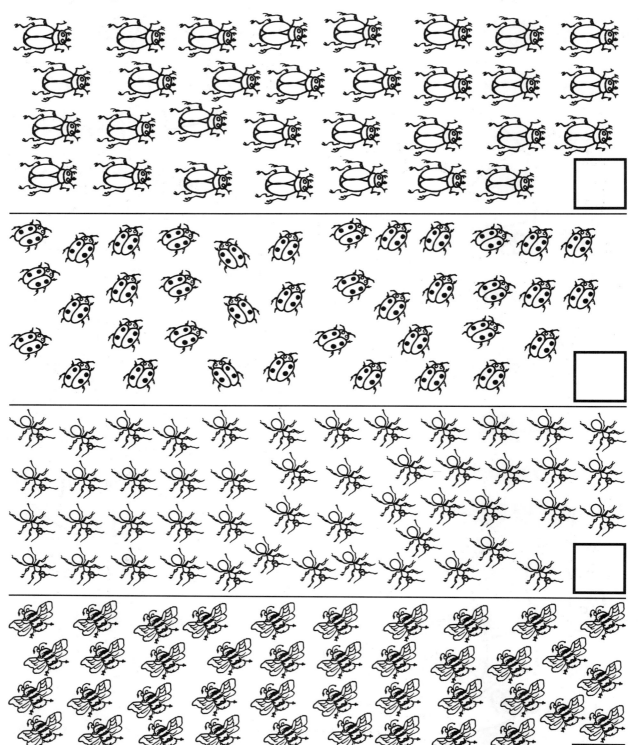

 Draw 50 ◯ circles.

Well done!

12

Numbers to 50: Counting

Name _____

Colour 41 ◯ circles red. Colour 39 ▢ squares blue.

Colour 50 △ triangles yellow.

 Draw 50 ◯ circles.

Well done!

 **13**

Numbers to 50: Ordering

Name _____

Colour the highest number in each group red.

 List the numbers from each group in order, lowest first.

Well done!

14

Numbers to 50: Ordering

Name _____

Put the soldiers in order, lowest first.

1. 17, 34, 26 →

2. 41, 29, 14 →

3. 31, 25, 49 →

4. 24, 50, 47 →

5. 45, 37, 48 →

 List all the soldiers in lines 1 and 2 in order.
List all the soldiers in lines 3 and 4 in order, then 4 and 5.

Well done!

15

Numbers to 50: Counting on

Name _____

How many?

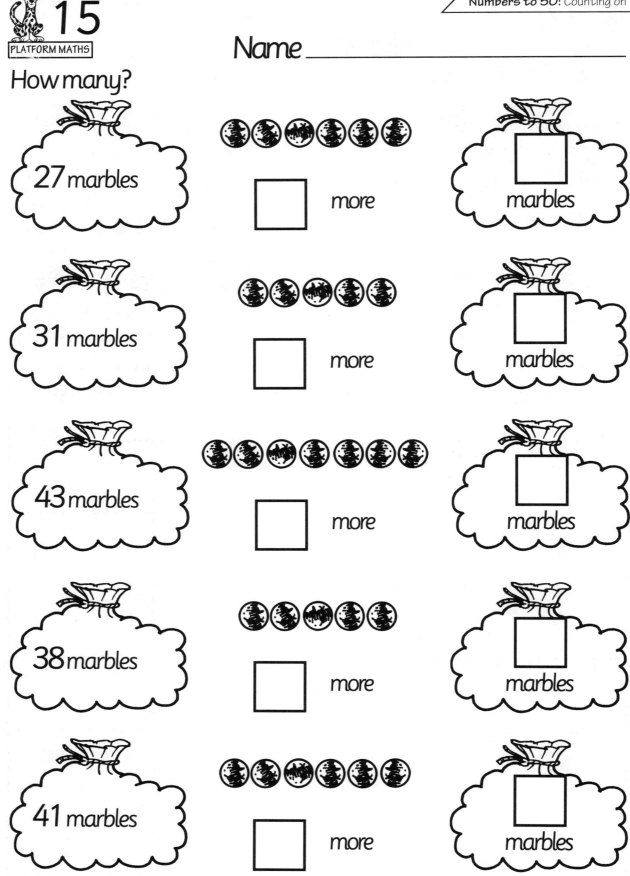

27 marbles — ☐ more — ☐ marbles

31 marbles — ☐ more — ☐ marbles

43 marbles — ☐ more — ☐ marbles

38 marbles — ☐ more — ☐ marbles

41 marbles — ☐ more — ☐ marbles

 Start on 29. Count on 7. End on ☐.
Start on 29 each time. Count on 9, 11, 14, 16. Where do you end up each time?

Well done!

 **16**

Name _____

Numbers to 50: Counting On

Where do you end up?

Start on 42   move on 7   end on ▢

Start on	move on	end on
40	8	
38	7	
41	6	
39	9	
38	12	
39	11	

 Copy the table but start on 37 each time. Where do you end up?

Well done!

17

Numbers to 50: Counting back

Name _____

How many?

Jar	Sweets taken out	Left
45 sweets	44 43 — take out ☐	☐ left
47 sweets	46 — take out ☐	☐ left
41 sweets	40 — take out ☐	☐ left
35 sweets	34 — take out ☐	☐ left
42 sweets	take out ☐	☐ left

Start with 50  sweets. Take out different numbers of sweets. How many left each time? Do this 8 times.

Well done!

Numbers to 50: Counting back

Name _____

Where do you end up?

Start on 50   count back 7   end on ☐

Start on	count back	end on
49	9	
48	7	
46	8	
47	6	
44	10	
48	11	
49	11	

 Copy the table but start on 50 each time. What do you end on?

Well done!

19

Pre-multiplication: Counting on

Name _____

Colour the numbers the frog lands on.

1	2	3	4	5	6	7	8	9	10
11	12	13	14	15	16	17	18	19	20

Jump in 2s

1	2	3	4	5	6	7	8	9	10
11	12	13	14	15	16	17	18	19	20

Jump in 2s

1	2	3	4	5	6	7	8	9	10
11	12	13	14	15	16	17	18	19	20

Jump in 3s

1	2	3	4	5	6	7	8	9	10
11	12	13	14	15	16	17	18	19	20

Jump in 5s

 Try your own jumps on a number grid or number line.

Well done!

20

Pre-multiplication: Grouping

Name _____

How many? Ring the sets.

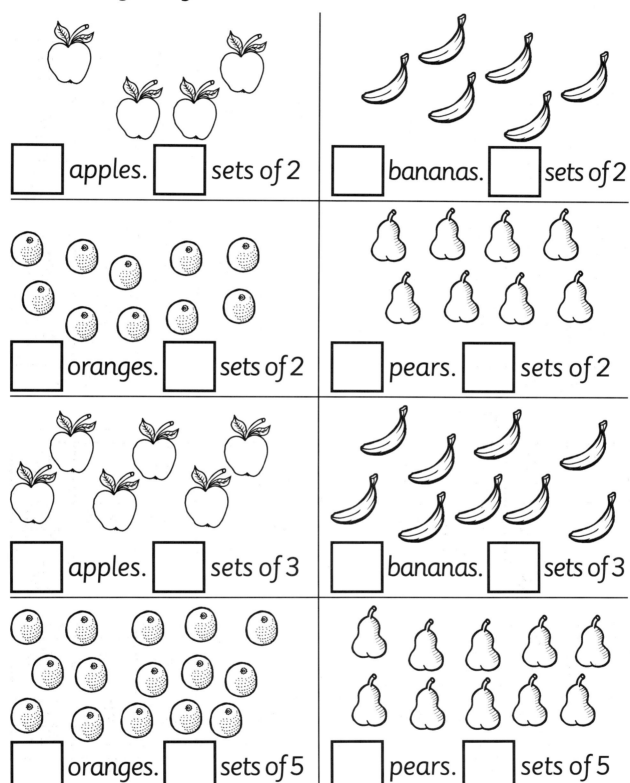

☐ apples. ☐ sets of 2	☐ bananas. ☐ sets of 2
☐ oranges. ☐ sets of 2	☐ pears. ☐ sets of 2
☐ apples. ☐ sets of 3	☐ bananas. ☐ sets of 3
☐ oranges. ☐ sets of 5	☐ pears. ☐ sets of 5

 Put 12 ☐ cubes in sets of 2, sets of 3, sets of 4 and sets of 6.
Put 10 cubes in sets of 2 and sets of 5.

Well done!

21

Pre-division: Counting back

Name _____

Colour the numbers the owl lands on.

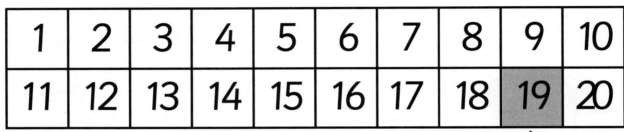

Fly back in 2s.

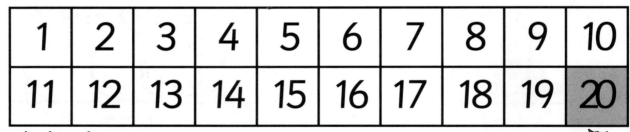

Fly back in 2s.

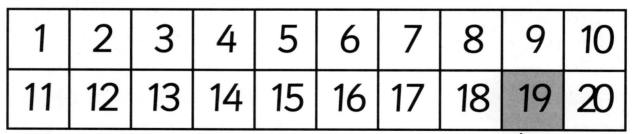

Fly back in 5s.

1	2	3	4	5	6	7	8	9	10
11	12	13	14	15	16	17	18	19	20

Fly back in 3s.

 Try your own moves on a number grid or number line.

Well done!

Pre-division: Sharing

Name _____

Share equally. Join the bones to the dogs.

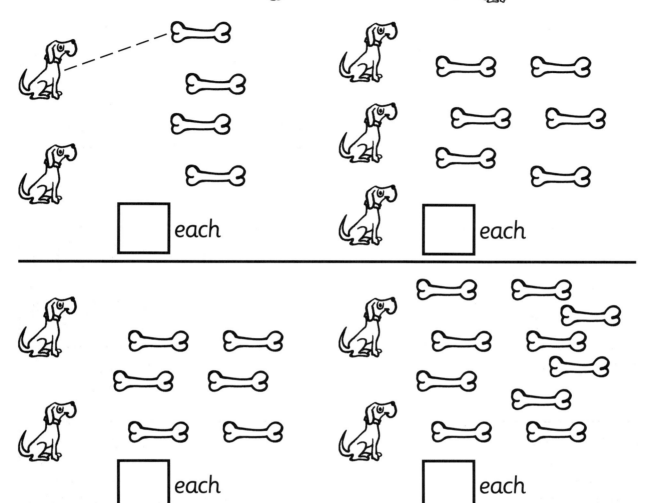

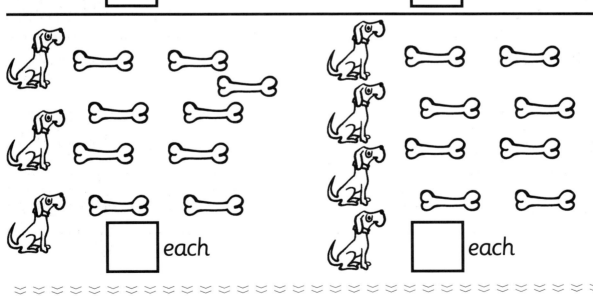

 You have 12 bones. Share them between 2 dogs, 3 dogs, 4 dogs and 6 dogs.

Well done!

23

Extending patterns: What comes next?

Name _____

What comes next?

1 2 1 2 1 2 ☐

1 2 3 1 2 3 1 2 ☐

1 2 2 1 2 2 1 2 2 ☐

1 3 1 3 1 3 1 3 1 ☐

3 4 5 3 4 5 3 4 5 ☐

2 3 3 2 3 3 2 3 3 ☐

4 5 4 5 4 5 4 5 4 ☐

2 2 3 3 2 2 3 3 2 ☐

 Make some patterns of your own.

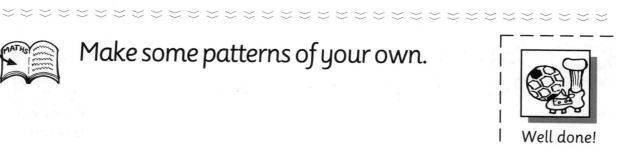

Well done!

24

Extending patterns: What comes next?

Name _____

What comes next?   **Circle the right one.**

Draw some patterns of your own.

Well done!

25

Name _____

Number sequences: Counting in 2s

Count in 2s. Colour the numbers.

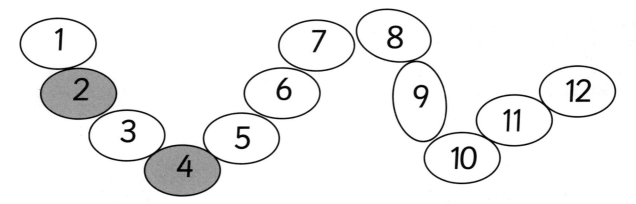

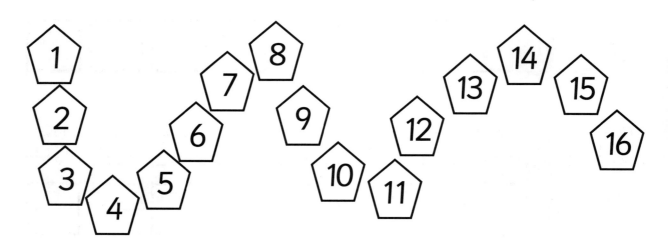

Draw a number grid up to 20.
Colour the sequence of 2s.

Well done!

 **26**

Number sequences: Counting in 2s

Name _____

Count in 2s. How many altogether?

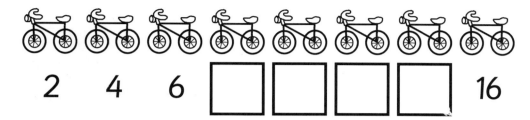

2   4   6   ☐ ☐ ☐ ☐   16

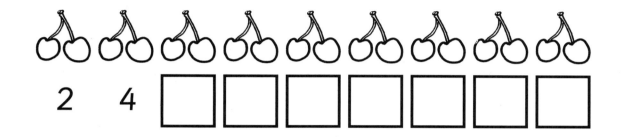

2   4   ☐ ☐ ☐ ☐ ☐ ☐ ☐

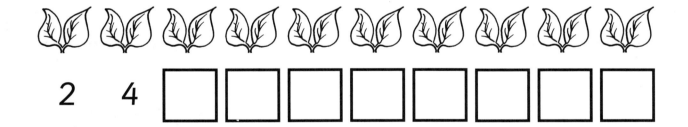

2   4   ☐ ☐ ☐ ☐ ☐

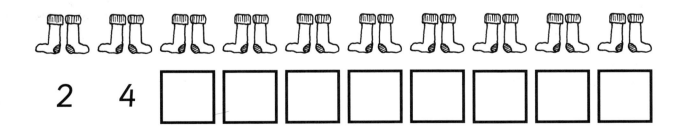

2   4   ☐ ☐ ☐ ☐ ☐ ☐ ☐ ☐

2   4   ☐ ☐ ☐ ☐ ☐ ☐ ☐ ☐

 Draw some sequences of 2.

Well done!

 **27**

Number sequences: Counting in 2s

Name _____

Fill in the missing numbers on the '2' snakes.

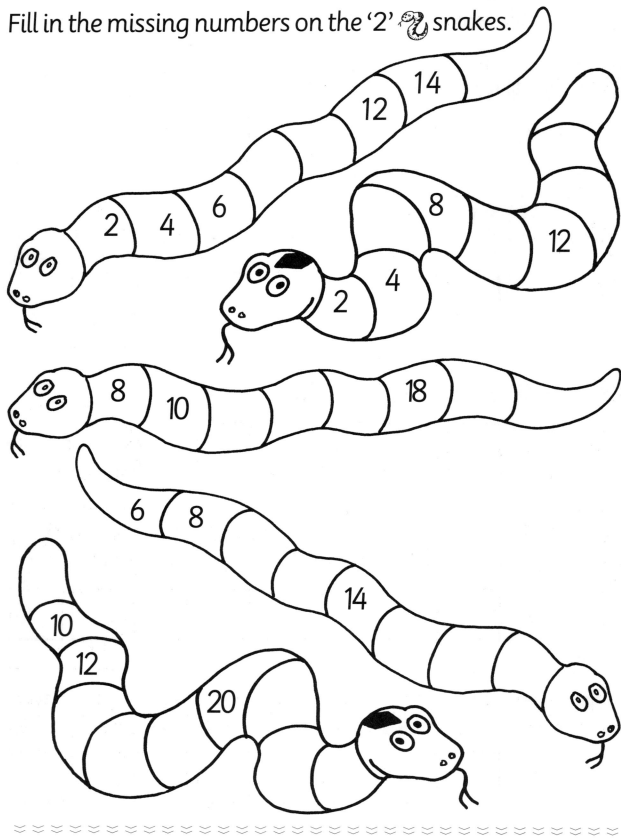

 Draw a '2' snake from 2 to 12.

Draw a '2' snake from 10 to 20.

Well done!

 **28**

Name _____

Number sequences: Multiples of 2

Count in 2s. Colour the odd one out in each row.

 4  10  12  17

 6  11  14  16

 7  18  20  22

 24  19  16  12

 20  18  14  15

List the 2s between 7 and 15,
11 and 25,
3 and 17.

Well done!

 **29**

Name _____

Number sequences: Counting in 5s

Count in 5s. Colour the numbers.

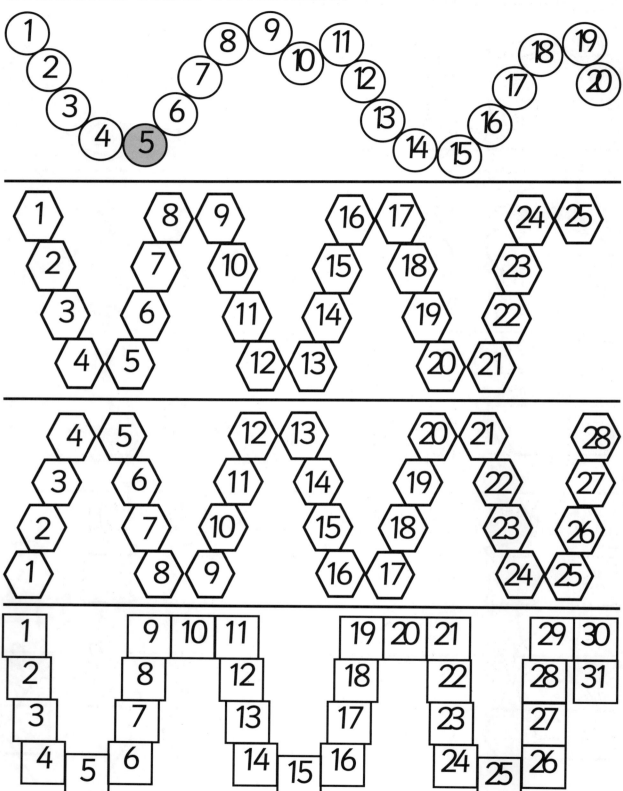

 Draw a number grid up to 50.
Colour the sequence of 5s.

Well done!

 **30**

Number sequences: Counting in 5s

Name _____

Count in 5s. How many altogether?

| 5 | 10 | 15 | ☐ |

   flower flower
| 5 | 10 | ☐ | ☐ | ☐ |

     seed
| 5 | ☐ | ☐ | ☐ | ☐ | ☐ |

| 5 | ☐ | ☐ | ☐ | ☐ | ☐ | ☐ |

| 5 | ☐ | ☐ | ☐ | ☐ | ☐ | ☐ | ☐ |

Draw some sequences of 5.

Well done!

31

Name _____

Fill in the missing numbers on the 5 S scarves.

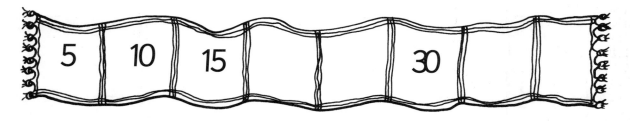

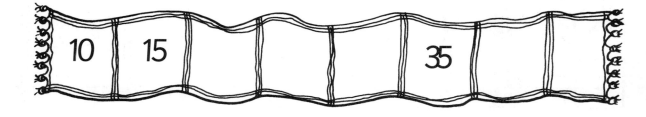

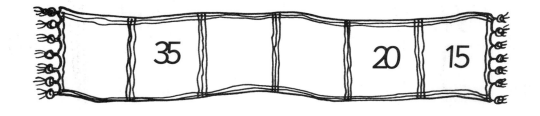

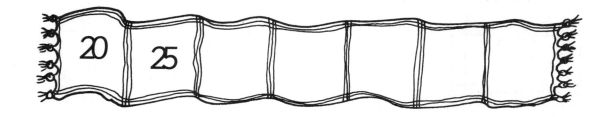

Draw a 5 S scarf from 5 to 25.

Draw a 5 S scarf from 30 to 50.

Well done!

32

Number sequences: Multiples of 5

Name _____

Count in 5s. Colour the odd one out in each row.

10	17	15	20
25	5	12	30
29	15	20	40
45	5	30	37
35	50	46	40

List the 5s between 9 and 26,
24 and 46,
0 and 31.

Well done!

33

Number sequences: Multiples of 2 and 5

Name _____

Colour the 2s red. Colour the 5s blue.

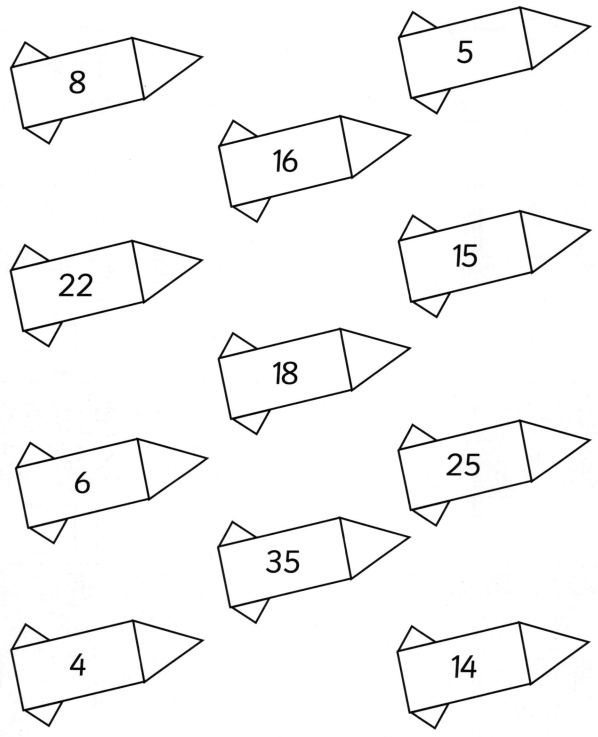

Draw two more '2' rockets.

Draw one more '5' rocket.

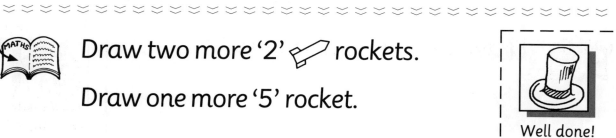

Well done!

34

Number sequences: Counting in 10s

Name _____

Count in 10s. How many altogether?

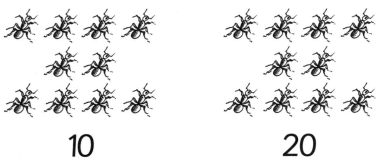
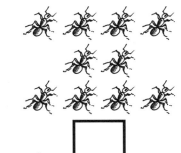

10   20   ☐

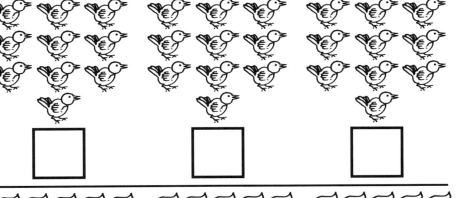

10   ☐   ☐   ☐

10   ☐   ☐   ☐

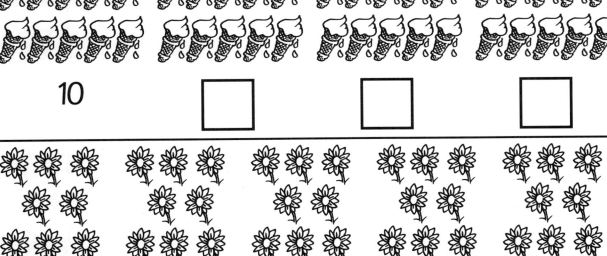

10   ☐   ☐   ☐   ☐

 Draw some sequences of 10.

Well done!

 **35**

Count in 10s.

Name _____

Number sequences: Counting in 10s

1 box has 10 eggs.	1 dinosaur has 10 scales.
2 boxes have 20 eggs.	2 dinosaurs have ☐
3 boxes have ☐	3 dinosaurs have ☐
4 boxes have ☐	4 dinosaurs have ☐
5 boxes have ☐	5 dinosaurs have ☐
1 caterpillar has 10 stripes.	1 flag has 10 stars.
2 caterpillars have ☐	2 flags have ☐
3 caterpillars have ☐	3 flags have ☐
4 caterpillars have ☐	4 flags have ☐
5 caterpillars have ☐	5 flags have ☐
1 robot has 10 teeth.	1 bag has 10 sweets.
2 robots have ☐	2 bags have ☐
3 robots have ☐	3 bags have ☐
4 robots have ☐	4 bags have ☐
5 robots have ☐	5 bags have ☐

 1 ladybird has 10 spots.
How many spots on 2, 3, 4 and 5 ladybirds?

Well done!

Addition to 20: Adding units

Name _____

How many?

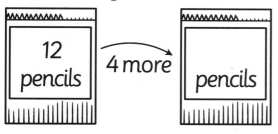 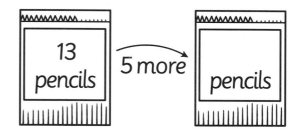

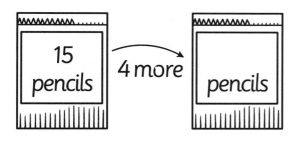 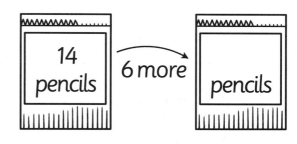

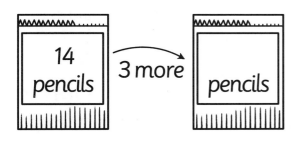 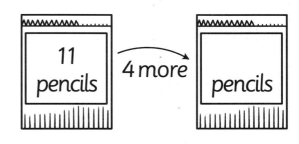

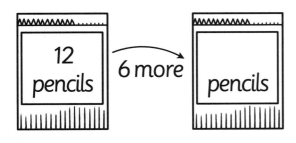 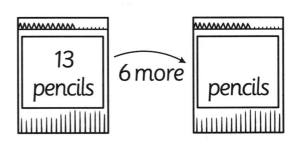

 You need 20 ☐ cubes. Start with 12. Add some more. How many altogether? Do this 6 times. Try a new start number.

Well done!

37

Addition to 20: Adding units

Name _____

Colour the leaves to match the right tree.

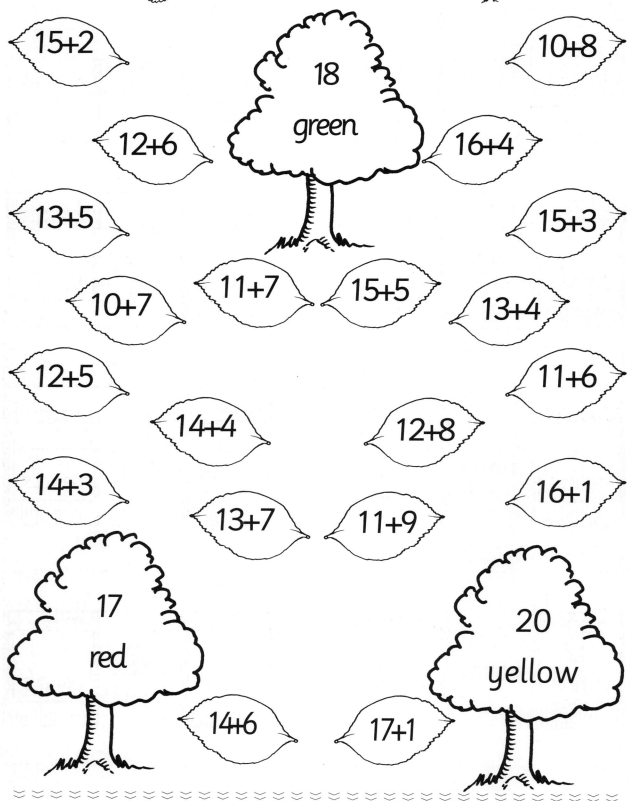

 Draw 5 leaves for a 19 tree.
Draw 3 leaves for a 16 tree.

Well done!

 **38**

Addition to 20: Adding 10

Name _____

Where does the worm end up?

| 1 | 2 | 3 | 4 | 5 | 6 | 7 | 8 | 9 | 10 | 11 | 12 | 13 | 14 | 15 | 16 | 17 | 18 | 19 | 20 |

Start on 6   slide 10   end on ☐

| 1 | 2 | 3 | 4 | 5 | 6 | 7 | 8 | 9 | 10 | 11 | 12 | 13 | 14 | 15 | 16 | 17 | 18 | 19 | 20 |

Start on	slide	end on
8	10	
4	10	
9	10	
7	10	
10	10	
5	10	
2	10	

 Make a number strip 1-20. Colour the 3 red. Add 10. Colour the answer red. Use different colours to do 5 more add 10 sums.

Well done!

 **39**

Addition to 20: Adding 10

Name _____

Add 10 to each 👕 shirt. Match to the right 👖 trousers.

5 12 6

8 15 2

14 18 9 16

19 4 7

10 20 17

 You need ⬚ - ⬚ cards.
Pick a card. Add 10.
Do this 7 times.

Well done!

 **40**

Addition to 20: Over the 10 boundary

Name _____

Colour houses that make 17 red, 16 blue, 15 yellow, 14 green.

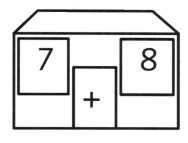
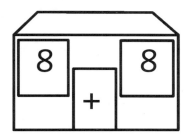
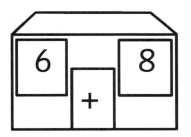
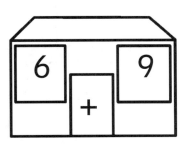
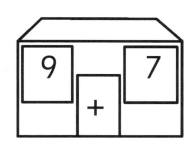
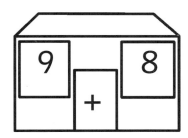
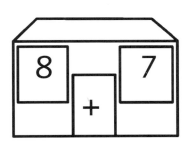
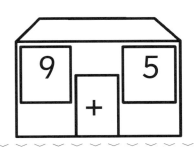
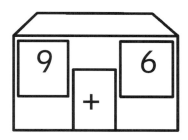
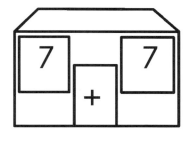
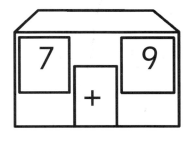
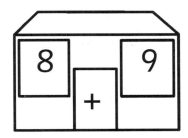

 Draw four houses that make 13.
Draw four houses that make 12.

Well done!

41

Addition to 20: Over the 10 boundary

Name _____

Colour only 2 ◯ balls in each ▢ box. They must make the total shown.

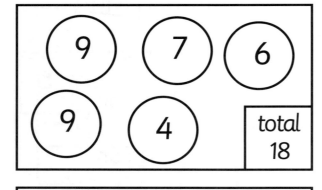
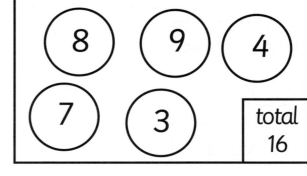
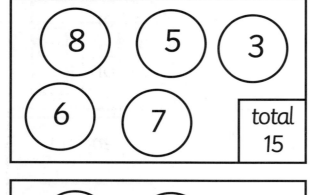
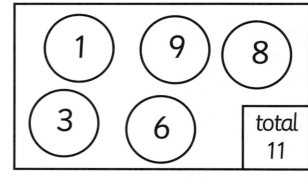
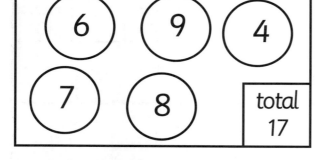
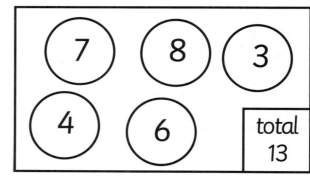
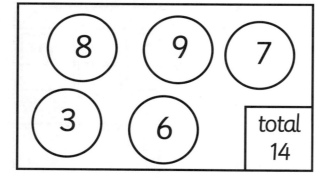
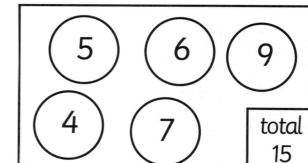

List 4 pairs of numbers that make 15.
List 4 pairs of numbers that make 17.

Well done!

Subtraction to 20: Subtracting units

Name _____

Where does the 🦛 hippo end up?

| 1 | 2 | 3 | 4 | 5 | 6 | 7 | 8 | 9 | 10 | 11 | 12 | 13 | 14 | 15 | 16 | 17 | 18 | 19 | 20 |

Start on 18   walk back 5   end on ☐

Start on 18   walk back 8   end on ☐

Start on 18   walk back 6   end on ☐

Start on 18   walk back 4   end on ☐

Start on	walk back	end on
🦛 17	4	
🦛 17	6	
🦛 17	3	
🦛 17	5	
🦛 17	2	
🦛 17	7	

 Copy out the table but start on 19.
Do it again but start on 20.

Well done!

43

Subtraction to 20: Subtracting units

Name _____

How many left?

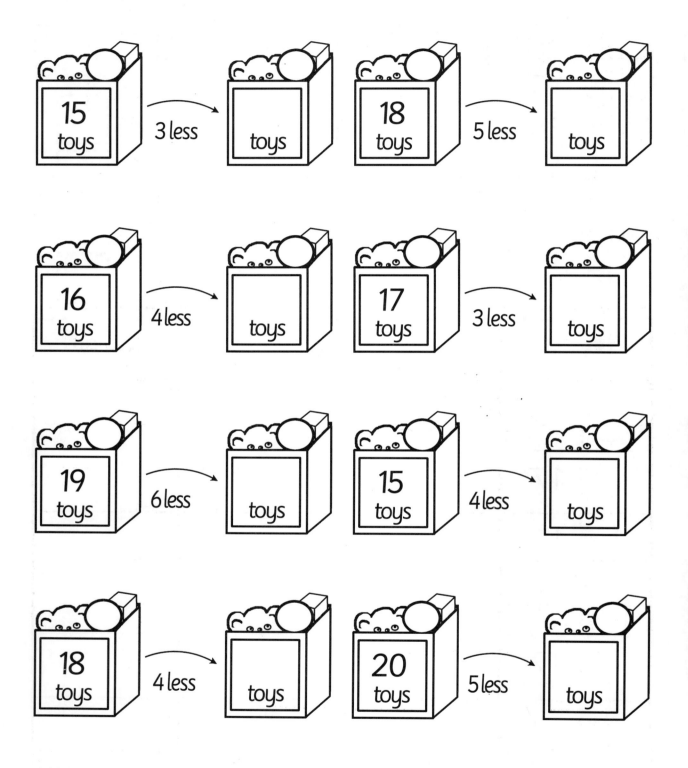

Start with 18 cubes. Take some away. How many left? Do this 6 times:

Take away ☐   ☐ **left.**

Well done!

 **44**

Name _____

Subtraction to 20: Subtracting 10

Where does the train end up?

| 1 | 2 | 3 | 4 | 5 | 6 | 7 | 8 | 9 | 10 | 11 | 12 | 13 | 14 | 15 | 16 | 17 | 18 | 19 | 20 |

Start on 19   chuff back 10   end on ☐

| 1 | 2 | 3 | 4 | 5 | 6 | 7 | 8 | 9 | 10 | 11 | 12 | 13 | 14 | 15 | 16 | 17 | 18 | 19 | 20 |

Start on	chuff back	end on
14	10	
17	10	
12	10	
11	10	
20	10	
16	10	
19	10	
15	10	

 Make a number strip 1-20. Colour 19 red. Take away 10. Colour the answer red. Do 4 more 'take 10' sums.

Well done!

 **45**

Subtraction to 20: Subtracting 10

Name _____

How many left?

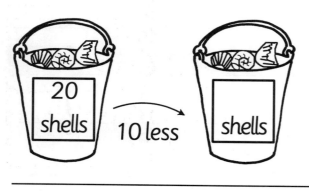

 List your answers like this:

17-10=☐   13-10=☐

46

Subtraction to 20: Over the 10 boundary

Name _____

Work out the sums. Colour the odd one out in each row.

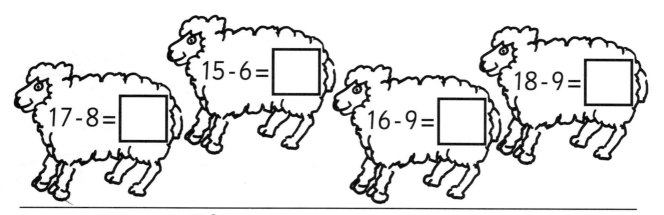

17 - 8 =   15 - 6 =   16 - 9 =   18 - 9 =

16 - 8 =   14 - 6 =   15 - 8 =   17 - 9 =

14 - 7 =   16 - 9 =   13 - 7 =   15 - 8 =

12 - 7 =   15 - 9 =   14 - 8 =   13 - 7 =

Start with 16 each time. Take away 7.
Take away 8. Take away 9.
Now start with 15.

Well done!

 **47**

Subtraction to 20: Over the 10 boundary

Name _____

Work out the sum on each door. Colour the correct window.

 Draw 4 houses with 8 as the answer.
Draw 4 houses with 9 as the answer.

Well done!

48

Addition to 20: Number facts

Name _____

Colour the sums that make 20.

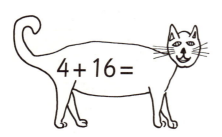 4 + 16 =
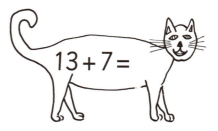 15 + 5 =
13 + 7 =

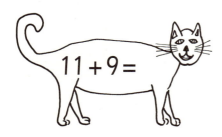 11 + 9 =
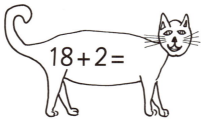 18 + 2 =
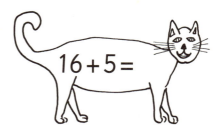 16 + 5 =

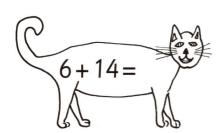 6 + 14 =
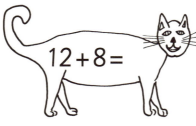 12 + 8 =
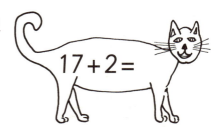 17 + 2 =

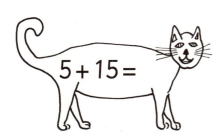 5 + 15 =
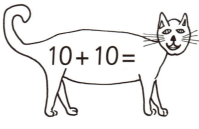 10 + 10 =
 19 + 1 =

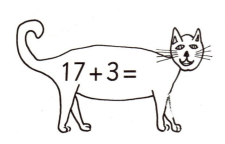 17 + 3 =
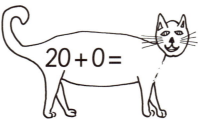 20 + 0 =
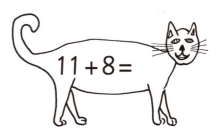 11 + 8 =

List ten sums that make 20.

Well done!

 **49**

Addition to 20: Number facts

Name _____

Match to make 20.

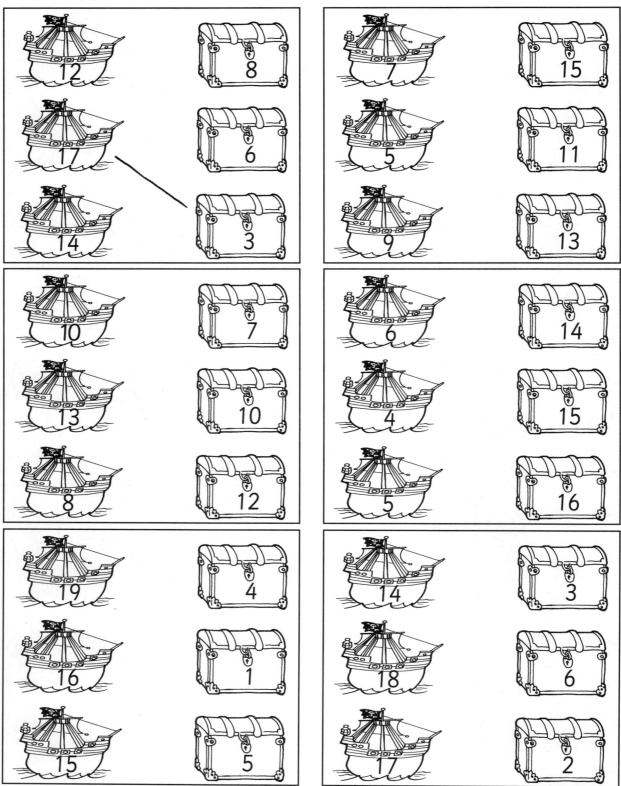

 Pick 6 numbers less than 20. Make each number up to 20. Write your answers like this: ☐ + ☐ = 20

Well done!

50
PLATFORM MATHS

Addition to 20: Number facts

Name_____

Work out the sums. Colour the odd one out in each row.

Row 1: 14+6 = ☐   11+9 = ☐   15+4 = ☐   17+3 = ☐

Row 2: 15+5 = ☐   18+2 = ☐   12+8 = ☐   14+7 = ☐

Row 3: 16+4 = ☐   11+8 = ☐   13+7 = ☐   15+5 = ☐

Row 4: 14+7 = ☐   17+3 = ☐   12+8 = ☐   11+9 = ☐

Row 5: 20+0 = ☐   16+3 = ☐   19+1 = ☐   2+18 = ☐

 List nine sums that make 19.

Well done!

 **51**

Subtraction to 20: Number facts

Name _____

Colour the ☐ funnel with the right answer.

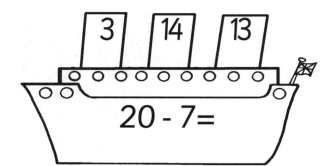
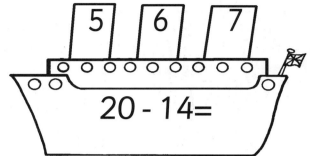
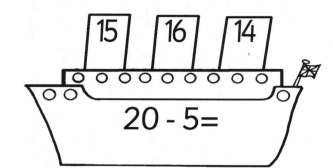
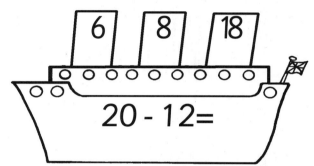
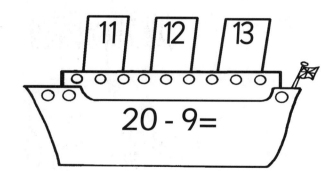
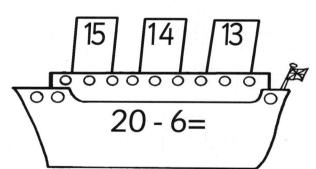
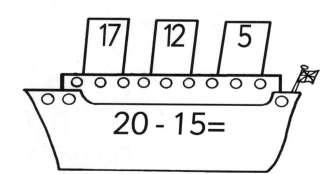
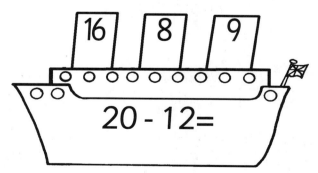

 Start with 20 each time.
Write 8 different subtraction sums:

20 - ☐ = ☐

 **52**

Subtraction to 20: Number facts

Name _____

Colour the correct sums.

20 - 4 = 6

20 - 7 = 13

20 - 5 = 14

20 - 11 = 9

20 - 12 = 8

20 - 17 = 4

20 - 15 = 6

20 - 8 = 12

20 - 10 = 10

20 - 3 = 18

20 - 16 = 4

20 - 6 = 14

20 - 9 = 11

 Copy this and fill it in in ten different ways:

20 - ☐ = ☐

Well done!

53

PLATFORM MATHS

Subtraction to 20: Number facts

Name _____

How many left?

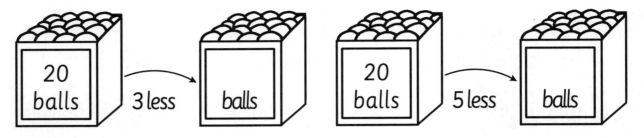

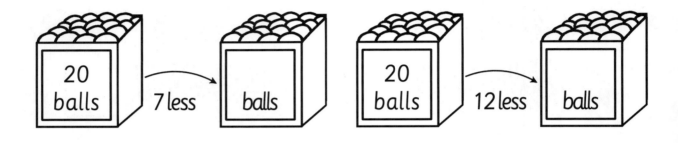

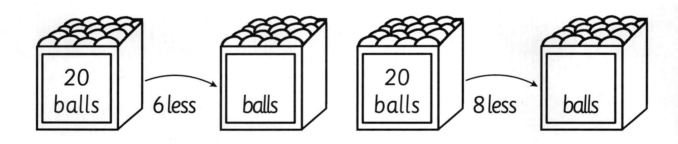

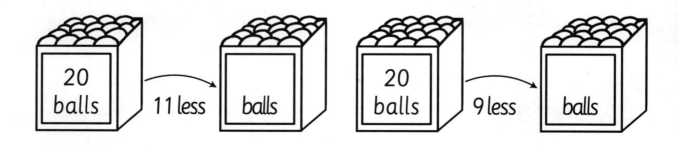

You need [0]-[9] cards. Start on 20 each time. Pick a card and take it away.

Well done!

54

Name _____

Place Value: Up to 19

Colour 10. How many spiders on each string?

☐ spiders

☐ spiders

☐ spiders

☐ spiders

☐ spiders

☐ spiders

 List your answers like this:

10 and 5 make ☐

Well done!

 **55**

Place Value: Up to 19

Name _____

There are 10 chips in each bag. How many chips altogether?

☐ chips	☐ chips
☐ chips	☐ chips
☐ chips	☐ chips
☐ chips	☐ chips

 List your answers like this:

☐ is 10 and 3.

Well done!

56

Name _____

Place Value: Up to 19

Colour 10. How many altogether?

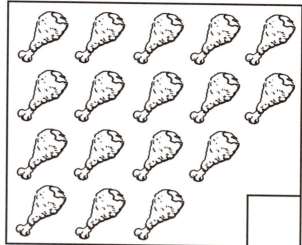

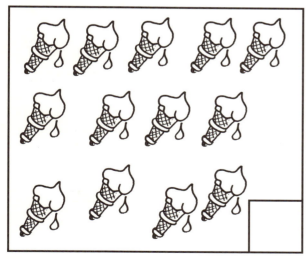

Complete this sentence in 6 ways:

10 ☐ and ☐ makes ☐

Well done!

57

Name_____

Place Value: Up to 19

Each △ is 10. Each ☐ is 1. So △☐☐☐ makes 13.
Colour to show the number in the box.

12	17
14	17
11	19
18	15

 If ○ is 10 and ☐ is 1 show the numbers 5, 11, 14, 19, and 16.

Well done!

58

Place Value: Up to 50

Name_____

How many? Each △ is 10. Each ○ is 1.

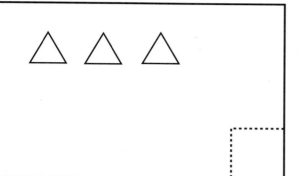
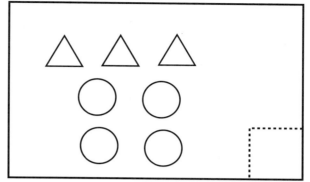
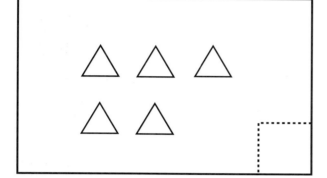
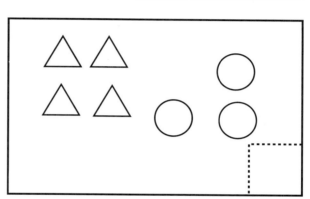
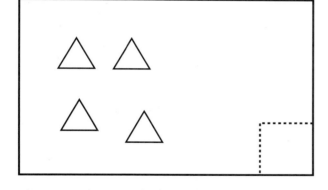
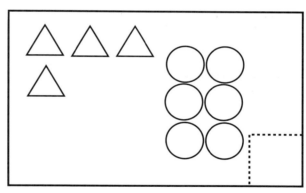
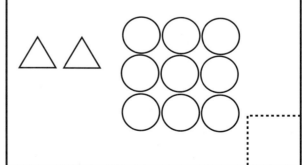

Draw these numbers: 17, 26, 32, 45, 25, 19.

Well done!

 **59**

Place Value: Up to 50

Name_____

How many coins in the bag to make the total shown.

Total 16	Total 23
Total 44	Total 35
Total 28	Total 41
Total 37	Total 19

 27 is 20 and 7. List these numbers in the same way: 36, 42, 18, 25, 12 49.

Well done!

60

Place Value: Up to 50

Name _____

What is the digit in the cloud worth? (2)4 → 20

3(6) → ☐   4(2) → ☐

1(7) → ☐   3(6) → ☐

3(9) → ☐   3(2) → ☐

2(5) → ☐   4(7) → ☐

3(4) → ☐   1(2) → ☐

4(1) → ☐   3(8) → ☐

2(2) → ☐   4(9) → ☐

 List four numbers with the 2 worth 20.
List five numbers with the 4 worth 40.

Well done!

61

Number problems: Addition

Name _____

☐ tortoises   ☐ more   ☐ altogether

☐ penguins   ☐ more   ☐ altogether

☐ cakes   ☐ more   ☐ altogether

☐ fish   ☐ more   ☐ altogether

Draw to find out how many:

8 cakes   5 more   ☐ altogether

11 ladybirds   6 more   ☐ altogether

Well done!

Number problems: Addition

Name _____

Bill has 5 cakes. Bob has 7 more.

How many has Bob? ☐ + ☐ = ☐

John has 8 ducks. He buys 6 more.

How many ducks altogether? ☐ + ☐ = ☐

7 tadpoles in a pond. Put in 8 more.

How many tadpoles altogether? ☐ + ☐ = ☐

9 camels in a zoo. Add 7 more.

How many camels altogether? ☐ + ☐ = ☐

8 hedgehogs in a field. 9 more come.

How many hedgehogs now? ☐ + ☐ = ☐

7 birds in a park. 11 more fly in.

How many birds altogether? ☐ + ☐ = ☐

Add 7 more to each of these:
5 ducks, 8 cakes, 9 birds, 7 camels.
Write the sums.

Well done!

63

Name _____

Number problems: **Subtraction**

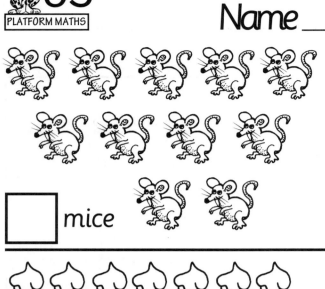

☐ mice   3 run away   ☐ left

☐ ice creams   eat 7   ☐ left

☐ tortoises   5 crawl away   ☐ left

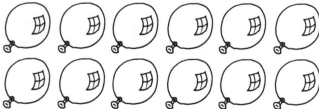

☐ balloons   8 pop   ☐ left

 I buy 12 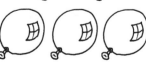 sweets. I eat 7. ☐ left

17  apples on a tree. 9 fall off. ☐ left

Well done!

64

Number problems: Subtraction

Name _____

Write a sum. How many left?

15 soldiers 8 march away ☐ - ☐ = ☐	14 apples 7 were eaten ☐ - ☐ = ☐
18 snakes 7 slide away ☐ - ☐ = ☐	17 ghosts 9 glide away ☐ - ☐ = ☐
19 ducks 8 swim away ☐ - ☐ = ☐	12 teddies 5 go to bed ☐ - ☐ = ☐
16 houses 9 fall down ☐ - ☐ = ☐	20 balloons 12 pop ☐ - ☐ = ☐

 How many left? **20 balloons. 6 pop.**
16 teddies. 4 go to bed.
19 apples. 13 eaten.

Well done!

65

Number problems: Addition and subtraction

Name _____

How many each time?

5 red cars   7 blue cars   ☐ + ☐ = ☐

7 green jars   11 brown jars   ☐ + ☐ = ☐

12 dogs   5 more dogs   ☐ + ☐ = ☐

13 fish   6 swim away   ☐ − ☐ = ☐

9 boats   6 sail away   ☐ − ☐ = ☐

11 pyramids   4 more built   ☐ + ☐ = ☐

16 starfish   9 crawl away   ☐ − ☐ = ☐

 Make up 6 number stories for ☐ + ☐ = ☐

Well done!

66

Name _____

Number problems: Addition and subtraction

How many each time? Write the sum and solve it.

10 skittles 8 fall down. How many are left? ▢ ○ ▢ = ▢	12 shells find 7 more. How many shells? ▢ ○ ▢ = ▢
James has 13 books. Mary has 5 more. How many altogether? ▢ ○ ▢ = ▢	18 plums in a bowl. 9 are bad. How many are good? ▢ ○ ▢ = ▢
14 hats 9 blow away. How many are left? ▢ ○ ▢ = ▢	11 pies eat 8. How many are left? ▢ ○ ▢ = ▢

Make up 6 number stories for

▢ - ▢ = ▢

Well done!

Numbers to 100: Ordering

Name _____

Colour the bee red which is 1 more than the hive.

Colour the bee blue which is 1 less than the hive.

 Write down the number of each bee you have not coloured. Draw a bee 1 less each time.

Well done!

68

Numbers to 100: Ordering

Name _____

Put the 🚌 buses in order. Lowest first.

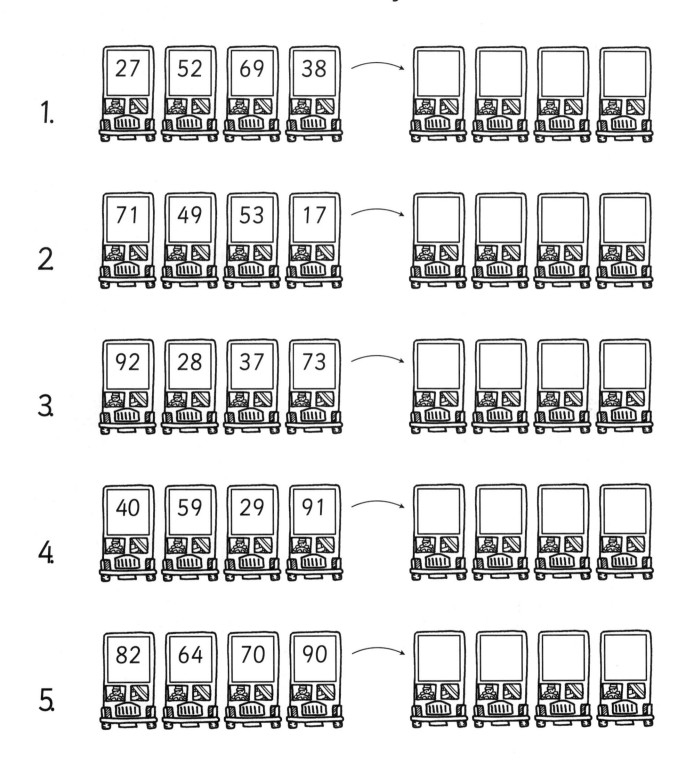

1. 27, 52, 69, 38
2. 71, 49, 53, 17
3. 92, 28, 37, 73
4. 40, 59, 29, 91
5. 82, 64, 70, 90

List the buses in rows 1 and 2 in order, highest first. List the buses in rows 3 and 4 in order, highest first.

Well done!

 **69**

Numbers to 100: Ordering

Name _____

Fill in the missing numbers.

1	2	3					8	9	
11		13			16			19	
21			24				28		30
	32				37				
41			44					49	
		53					58		
					66				
	72								80
		83					88		
91									

What's missing?

24	
34	

61	
	72

 Draw 6 grids like this: ⊞
Fill them in in different ways from the 1-100 grid.

Well done!

70

Numbers to 100: Ordering

Name _____

These pieces come from a 1-100 grid. Fill in the missing numbers.

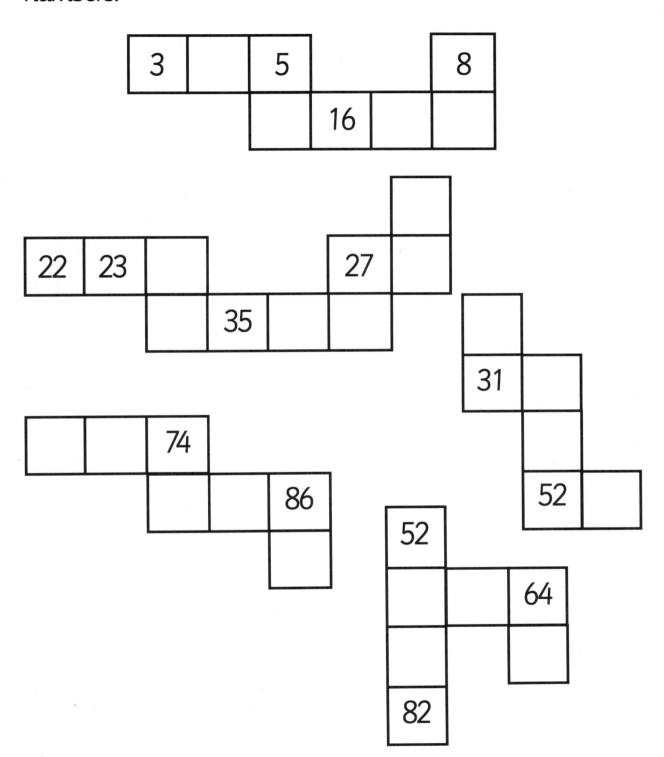

Copy the first shape 5 times. Fill it in in different ways.

Well done!

 71

Numbers to 100: Ordering

Name _____

Colour the rain drops to match their cloud.

Red More than 17 but less than 30

89, 50, 26, 20, 74, 39, 43, 19, 21, 41

Green More than 35 but less than 57

78, 40

Blue More than 72 but less than 97

76, 80, 55, 89

 List 5 rain drops for each of these clouds: More than 50 but less than 64
More than 81 but less than 92

Well done!

 **72**

Numbers to 100: Ordering

Name _____

Join the dots in order.

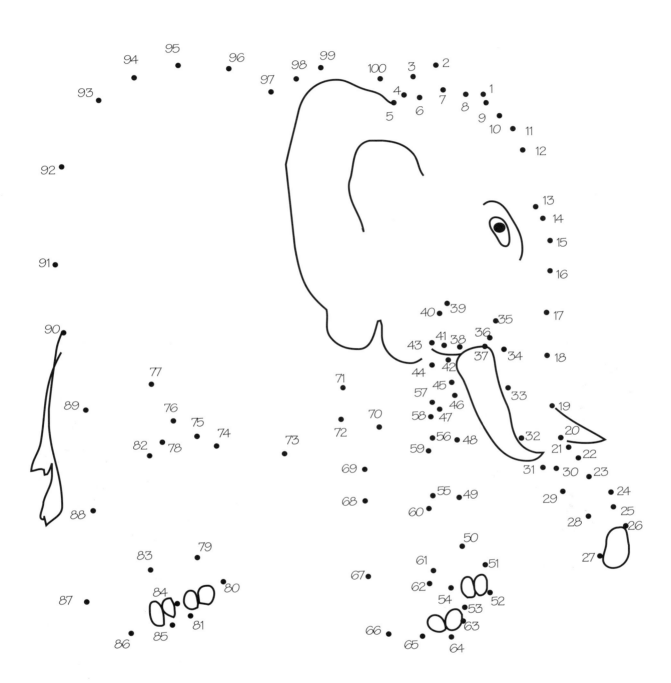

 List the next 10 numbers after each of these: 11, 39, 57, 76.

Well done!

73

Number sequences: Counting in 10s

Name _____

Fill in the missing numbers.

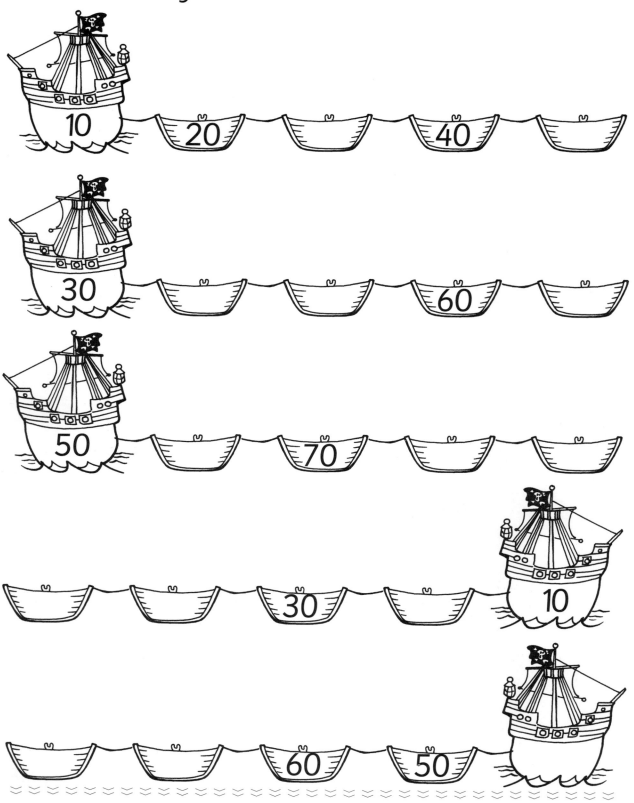

List the 10s from
20 to 80, 50 to 100, 90 to 30.

Well done!

 **74**

Number sequences: Counting in 10s

Name _____

Join the 10s in order.

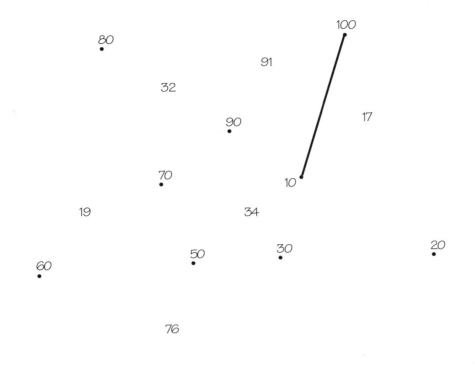

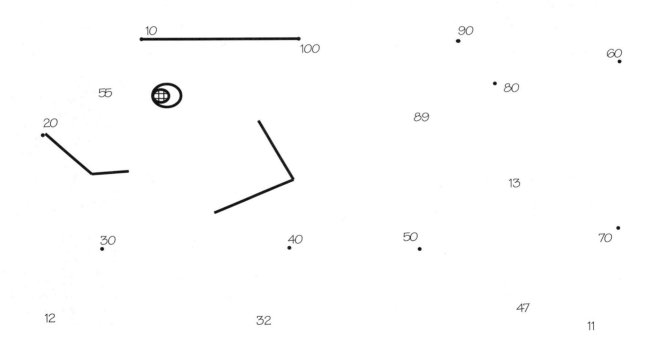

 Draw and join your own 10s dot to dot picture.

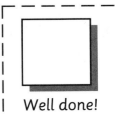
Well done!

 **75**

Number sequences: Multiples of 10

Name _____

Colour the 10s.

 Draw 3 new 10 trees.

Well done!

76

Place value: Up to 100

Name _____

Colour all the numbers with the units worth 4 in red.

1	2	3	4	5	6	7	8	9	10
11	12	13	14	15	16	17	18	19	20
21	22	23	24	25	26	27	28	29	30
31	32	33	34	35	36	37	38	39	40
41	42	43	44	45	46	47	48	49	50
51	52	53	54	55	56	57	58	59	60
61	62	63	64	65	66	67	68	69	70
71	72	73	74	75	76	77	78	79	80
81	82	83	84	85	86	87	88	89	90
91	92	93	94	95	96	97	98	99	100

List the numbers you have coloured:

Colour all the numbers with the units worth 7 in blue.

 List the blue numbers. What numbers would you colour if you started on 5?

Well done!

77

Name _____

Place Value: Up to 100

Colour the numbers with 5 tens blue, 6 tens red, 7 tens yellow.

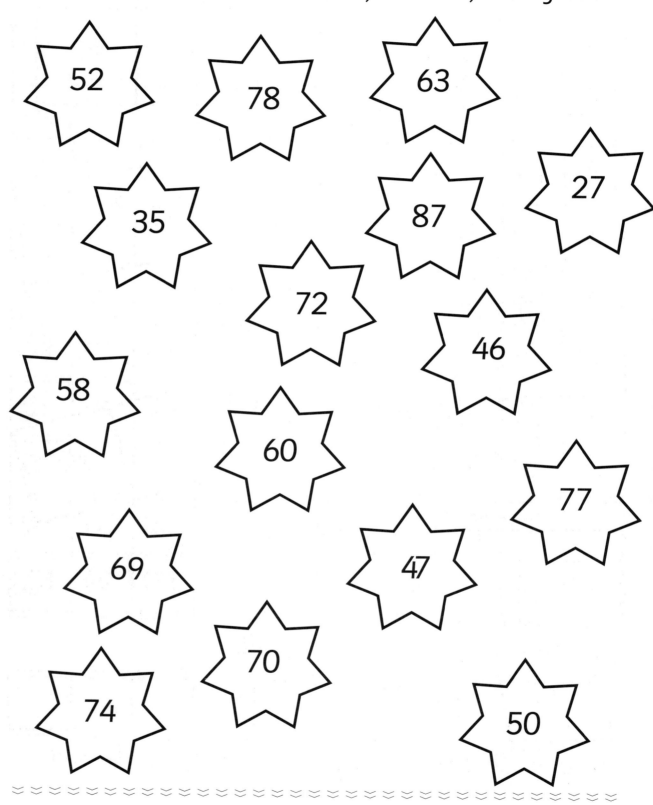

 List 5 more numbers for each colour.

Well done!

78

Place Value: Adding to 10

Name _____

Colour pairs with one number 10 more than the other.

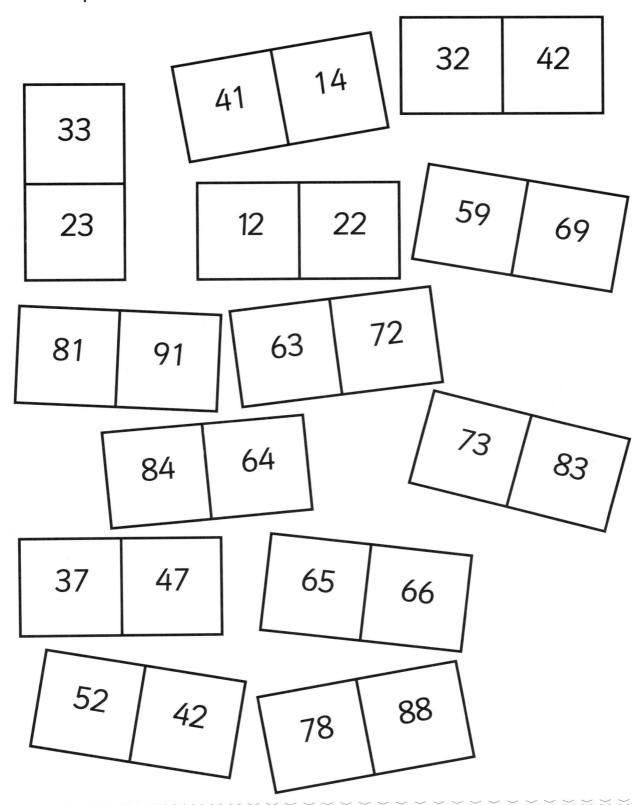

List the numbers you did not colour. Give each one a partner which is 10 more.

Well done!

 **79**

Place Value: Adding 10

Name _____

Add 10. Match to the answer.

20 → 30, 10, 25	30 → 33, 40, 50
60 → 50, 70, 65	80 → 90, 70, 89
40 → 60, 30, 50	10 → 21, 20, 11
70 → 80, 90, 71	50 → 69, 51, 60

 List your answers like this:
add 10
20 →

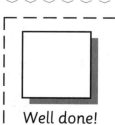
Well done!

Place Value: Adding 10

Name _____

Add 10 to the number in the middle. Colour the answer.

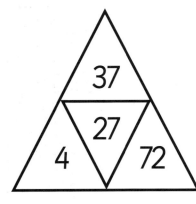
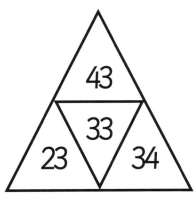
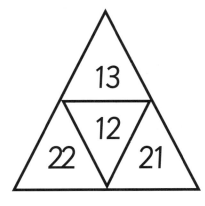
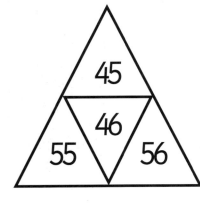
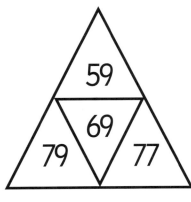
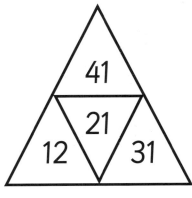
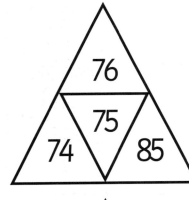
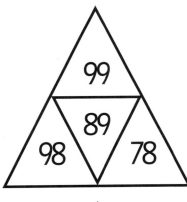
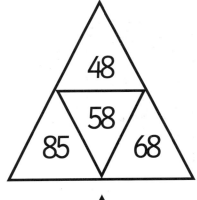
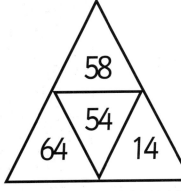
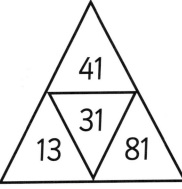
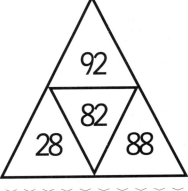

Pick a number you have not coloured. Add 10.
Do this for 10 numbers.

Well done!

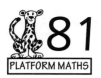

81

Place value: Taking 10

Name _____

Take away 10 from the monkey. Match to the right banana.

 Choose a banana from each group.

Take away 10. Write: ☐ −10 = ☐

Well done!

82

Name _____

Place value: Taking 10

Colour 96 red. Take away 10 and colour the answer red.

1	2	3	4	5	6	7	8	9	10
11	12	13	14	15	16	17	18	19	20
21	22	23	24	25	26	27	28	29	30
31	32	33	34	35	36	37	38	39	40
41	42	43	44	45	46	47	48	49	50
51	52	53	54	55	56	57	58	59	60
61	62	63	64	65	66	67	68	69	70
71	72	73	74	75	76	77	78	79	80
81	82	83	84	85	86	87	88	89	90
91	92	93	94	95	**96**	97	98	99	100

Take away 10 again. Keep going. List the numbers:

96									

Colour 92 blue. Keep taking 10 away.

List the blue numbers. What numbers would you colour if you started on 98?

Well done!

83

Place value: Difference

Name _____

Colour the ◆ kites with a difference of 10.

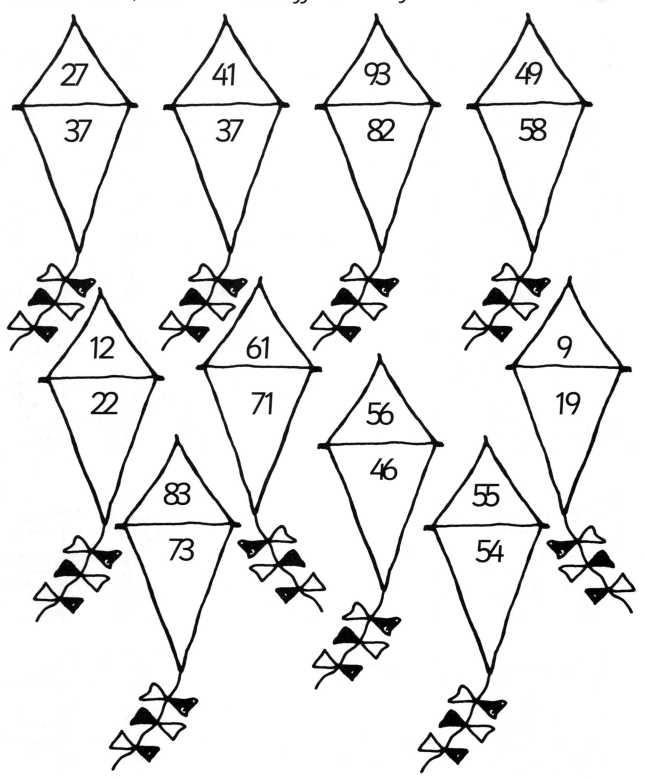

Draw 6 kites with a difference of 10.

Well done!

A
PLATFORM MATHS

Resource sheet

Name _____

Colour the odd one out in each row.

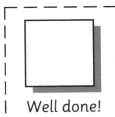

Well done!

B PLATFORM MATHS

Resource sheet

Name _____

Match the leaves to the right tree.

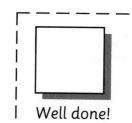

Well done!

C

Name _____

Resource sheet

Fill in the missing numbers.

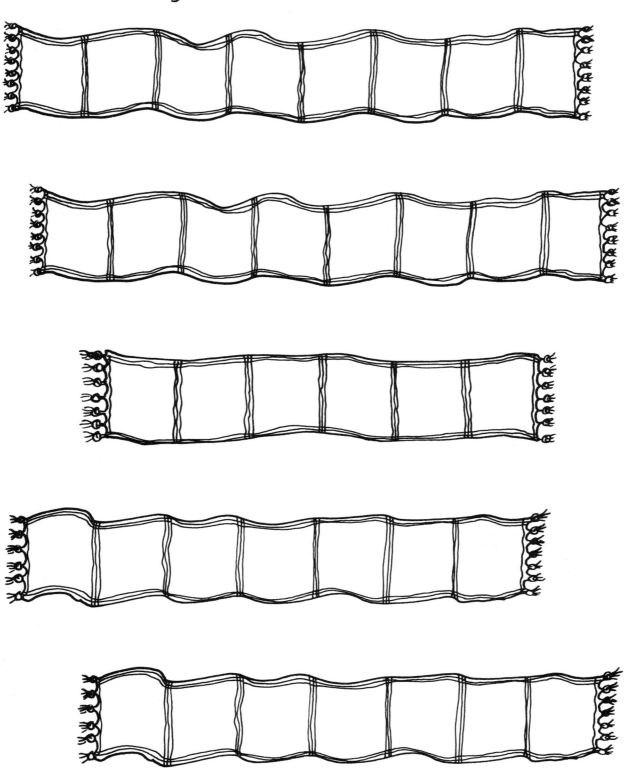

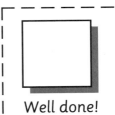

Well done!

D

Resource sheet

Name _____

Colour only 2 ◯ balls in each ☐ box. They must make the total shown.

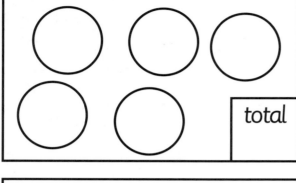
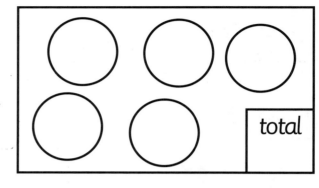
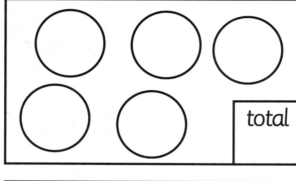
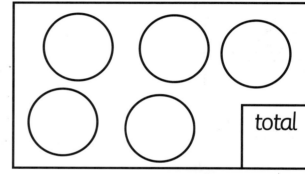
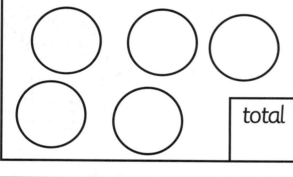
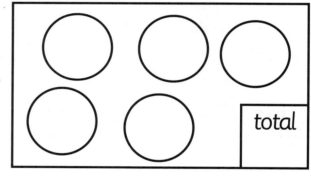
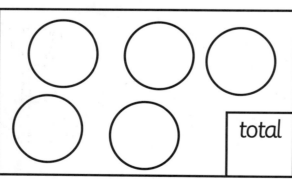
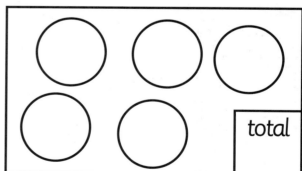

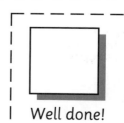

Well done!

E

Resources sheet

Name _____

How many

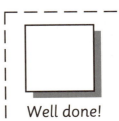

Well done!

F PLATFORM MATHS

Resource sheet

Name _____

Where do you end up?

| 1 | 2 | 3 | 4 | 5 | 6 | 7 | 8 | 9 | 10 | 11 | 12 | 13 | 14 | 15 | 16 | 17 | 18 | 19 | 20 |

Start on ☐   move ☐   end on ☐

Start on	move	end on

Well done!

G

Resource sheet

Name _____

Colour the houses that make:

red
blue
yellow

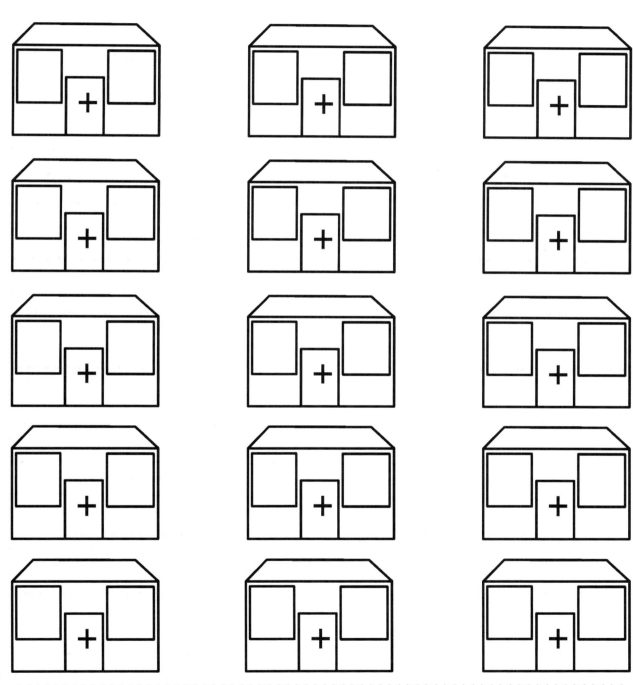

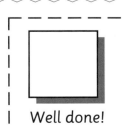

Well done!

H

Resource sheet

Name _____

1	2	3	4	5	6	7	8	9	10
11	12	13	14	15	16	17	18	19	20
21	22	23	24	25	26	27	28	29	30
31	32	33	34	35	36	37	38	39	40
41	42	43	44	45	46	47	48	49	50
51	52	53	54	55	56	57	58	59	60
61	62	63	64	65	66	67	68	69	70
71	72	73	74	75	76	77	78	79	80
81	82	83	84	85	86	87	88	89	90
91	92	93	94	95	96	97	98	99	100

Well done!